Time Thieves

The Ultimate Book On How To Stop People, Life, And Work From Stealing Your Precious Time Away.

MAHER ABIAD

Copyright © 2019 by Maher Abiad. All Rights Reserved.

No part of this publication may be reproduced, distributed, or transmitted in any form or by any means, including photocopying, recording, or other electronic or mechanical methods, or by any information storage and retrieval system without the prior written permission of the publisher, except in the case of very brief quotations embodied in critical reviews and certain other noncommercial uses permitted by copyright law.

ISBN-13: 978-1-0994-9383-6

CONTENTS

1	Why I Wrote This Book	Pg 1
2	Why You Must Read This Book	Pg 2
3	Time Thief 1: Social Media	Pg 4
4	Time Thief 2: Checking Email	Pg 7
5	Time Thief 3: Unplanned And Unsolicited Phone Calls	Pg 10
6	Time Thief 4: Not Saying No	Pg 13
7	Time Thief 5: Multitasking	Pg 16
8	Time Thief 6: Perfection	Pg 19
9	Time Thief 7: Busy Work	Pg 22
10	Time Thief 8: Not Delegating	Pg 24
11	Time Thief 9: Procrastination	Pg 28
12	Time Thief 10: Meetings	Pg 31
13	Time Thief 11: Endless To-Do Lists	Pg 34
14	Time Thief 12: Your 9 To 5 Job	Pg 37
15	Time Thief 13: Waiting In Traffic And Lineups	Pg 41
16	Time Thief 14: Having To Go Places	Pg 44
17	Time Thief 15: The News	Pg 47
18	About The Author	Pg 51

WHY I WROTE THIS BOOK

When I graduated high school, I had no idea what I wanted to do. I ended up bouncing from job to job, thing to thing, not knowing where my life was headed. Looking back, my 20's were a complete waste. If there were a time machine, I would go back in time and do things a lot differently.

One thing that has really hit me as I have gotten older, though, is that time is THE most precious resource we are given in our lives.

I wrote this book to highlight and really bring to peoples attention the one thing that most of us take for granted: Time itself - and how much of it we are throwing away and wasting.

I looked around, and I asked myself why some people can get so much accomplished in the exact same 24 hour day that we all have. While the majority of the population struggles with making any real progress day after day and as a whole in their lives.

When I started to live my life with a constant focus of time, I began to live a life entirely differently. I started to do things with more focus and efficiency; you could kind of say I started to treat time like it was gold. I began to hold on to it dear to my chest, protecting it with every ounce of power that I had.

And this is what will make you a real success in life and at work. This mindset and the teachings in this book will give you the tools to get more done because you are now using time to your advantage.

We all have 24 hours in a day, but we are all not using that 24 hours to our advantage. I didn't want to get older and have regrets by asking myself, "where did all my time go?"

Use every single tactic and strategy in this book to guide your life to true happiness, productivity, and the ultimate success.

WHY YOU MUST READ THIS BOOK

This book will help you if you are someone who knows your true worth. You understand that you can accomplish so much more in this world, support your family so much better, or even run your business more efficiently.

You are someone who is looking for the right tools and direction to take back control of your life.

As you are aware of the number of distractions that one faces from family, friends, and work, and you know that this amount of lost time is mind-boggling. With all the technology we have at our disposal, we are actually getting less done, and being much less productive than we used to.

There are many things you will discover in this book that will be eye-opening, and from there, you will know and be able to identify these areas in life and work where you can make drastic improvements on right away to get you on the right track.

This book is for those who want to be the best they can be and who understand that time can be used against you, or it can be used to help you. Unfortunately, most people throw away this extremely precious commodity that they are given, but by you taking the first step and reading this book, you are right away taking back control of your life and getting ahead of millions that are not.

You will take away life-changing methods and tactics to rewire your brain, the way you think, and the way you currently live your life. I want to offer you a blueprint that has dramatically helped me to take back control of my days and not let anything take away from the real things I need to do to grow as a person, and I hope you get the same and even better results.

Remember one thing throughout this book - your life is a straight line from birth to death. Throughout that time, people, commitments, situations, everything and anything will try to divert you from your path in life and your ultimate goals. You then end up living someone else's life and not yours. No matter what age you are now, I don't want you to have any regrets. I want to give you the strength and confidence through the teachings of this book to always be mindful of where you are going and what you need to do to get there.

TIME THIEF 1: SOCIAL MEDIA

To some, social media has been the best thing to fall upon them since sliced bread. To others, it's a thorn in their side. To you, it is something that you need to tread lightly, with caution, and the ultimate control.

How Social Media Is Being Used Today

I have been in digital media and marketing since 2000, and I have had my fair share of experience with social media for my own projects, as well as that of my clients.

There are literally billions of people all over the world daily surfing, posting, and using social media in some way or form.

From Facebook, Twitter, Pinterest, and Instagram, the amount of content being posted online could fill up an entire library in a day.

The great thing for these social media companies, is they do not need to generate or post any content of their own. They rely on people like you and me to be the content creators and do all the work for them.

Their Bigger Plan

If you boil it down, the social media companies primary goal is to sell ad space to advertisers. This is how they make money, through ad revenue that businesses pay them to put sponsored ads in front of a large group of people.

So it's the job of these social media companies to make their platforms addictive and to ensure that you stay on their platforms for as long as possible so that way you see more ads and click on them more often.

Casinos, for example, want you to play as long as possible, because at the end of the day, the longer you play, the more you lose to the house because the odds are stacked against players and in the house's favour. And because of this, you can draw a very similar line between the goal of a casino and the goal of a social media company.

Why It's A Good Idea To Tame It Down

So let's stop for a second and ask yourself exactly why you are using social media and spending so much time on it anyway?

You have most likely developed a habit of randomly checking social media apps when you are bored. Perhaps while you are waiting at a doctors office, sitting on the bus, or on breaks while at work.

Over time, this constant repetition has created a habit where you get a good release of dopamine in your brain when you get people to like your posts, for example.

Moderation is key to everything in life, if you need to jump on social media to post something of importance then get on and get off. If you are going to go on social media to just browse at what others are doing, then you are really not getting anything out of this.

The Solution To Breaking Free

Social media posts change daily and most of it won't matter in 20 years. Why would you throw away your time now, as it leaves your mind by the next day as new information piles into your feed and life? So ask yourself, what are you actually getting out of this form of entertainment?

Catch Yourself Before Going Onto Social Media

So the way to break any habit is to replace the thing you are trying to stop with something else. So for you to stop checking social media like your Facebook or Instagram feed when you are bored, catch yourself the next time you pull out your phone to press the app, and do something else that will actually benefit you in your life and get you either more financially free, in better shape and health, or improve a relationship with a friend or loved one.

The problem I find is that when you are bored, like sitting in a waiting room, you instinctively reach for your phone and open Facebook or Instagram. You have to catch yourself, and then ask what can I do instead of this.

Do Something That Will Benefit You Instead

Instead of watching something entertaining, learn a new language, learn a new skill you can use to make money, learn something instead that you can use to help others.

Because just like an hourglass, when that time is gone, and even if it's 5 minutes, that time is gone from your life. When you keep adding up 5 minutes here, 10 minutes there, daily, it adds up very quickly and all of a sudden you find you have wasted hours of time you could have used to move your life forward.

Randomly surfing things that will make no impact on your life is just a flat out waste of your most precious time. Even doing something good and helping someone else out would be more valuable than flipping through a Facebook feed.

TIME THIEF 2: CHECKING EMAIL

Email, loved by most, is actually misused and is taking away lots of precious time from you to be able to get your work done.

How Email Is Being Used Today

For many, they have their email wide open when they are working away on their desktops and have their notifications primed and ready to let them know when a new email comes in.

And when it does, they jump to the program right away to check who it is from, and what the person wants.

From there, they dive into the message to take action on what the other person has said and now spend time trying to come up with a reply, as well as drafting up a return message.

All while having completely stopped doing what they were doing before the email had arrived.

Why You Are Not Getting Much Done

The reason for why you are not getting much actual work done is simple, email is a reactive task that you engage in, which pushes and pulls you in many different directions that you may not have planned to go in.

For you to be successful and to get your time back, you have to plan your day out ahead of time, and methodically execute on your plan. Otherwise, if you just keep reacting to other peoples problems and issues when a new email and message comes in, then you are not living your life, you are living someone else's.

How You Should Be Using Email

First and foremost, don't have it open all the time, because you will always be in a "squirrel" like mode where the second the notification pops up saying you have a new email or message you go into reactive mode right away and stop what you are doing to react to what has come in.

Time Block When You Check

You need to create a dedicated time to check your email during the day.

And let me preface with something fundamental - do not check your emails first thing in the morning.

This is because you should have had your most important tasks for the morning planned out already, and if the first thing you are doing instead is reactive, then how do you expect to get anything done?

Someone's email can easily throw you off your game and get you then busy on something completely different, and from there, your entire day's plan is thrown out the door.

Create a block of time of 20 minutes once or twice a day to check your email, and that is it. Choose the exact same times every day and stick to that regiment. This could be something like 11am and 7pm, and that's it. You go in and get out. And when you get out, you are right back to your daily goals and tasks for the day.

Do you go to the post office every 5 minutes to check your paper mail? No, you don't. So why then has the addiction of checking email infected your life so much that it's created another habit of just reacting to what happens around your life instead of taking control.

You do not need to check your email every few minutes. This habit must be broken for you to fulfil your goals, protect your time, and get ahead in life and business.

Turn Off All Notifications

This one is crucial. For you to be able to focus on your work and get things actually done to completion, you need uninterrupted focus time.

So right now go to your phone and computer and turn off all notifications from showing up when an email comes in. Trust me on this one, you will find yourself being so much more productive when you can have that block of time just to work and be in a super deep focus to what you are doing.

Good luck trying to work when you have "dings" and "dongs" going off every few minutes. Your brain takes time to re-engage to what you are doing, so every time a notification comes in, you are prolonging yourself from going back into deep work.

So this goes for more than just email, turn off your notifications for email, messages, and social media as well, along with any other apps that you simply don't need to be disturbed from.

This will help you to be less reactive and more in control of your time and life.

Use Short Form

You are not writing university thesis papers here. You can use short form to get your message across quickly, such as 4 instead of four.

Using short form in your emails and messages will allow you to say what you need to say as quickly as possible and either move on to the next message or close down the program and get back to your deep work tasks.

This is especially helpful while using SMS text messaging to talk to some, as this example makes perfect sense, and gets the point across:

"i wil b ther in 20min, dont wait 4 me, go inside & resrve a table 4 us, thx c u soon."

A basic example, but you get the picture, time is passing by every second, no need to waste your time making things perfect if it makes no difference in the end.

Add Sent From My iPhone/Android

A neat little trick you can use is to put Sent from my iPhone/Android that way even if you send from desktop, people think you sent from your phone where it's much harder to type longer emails, and thus won't anticipate long-winded answers in your reply.

Another one is:

"- Sent from a mobile device. Excuse the brevity and typos."

The point here is this gives you a reason on why your reply was so short and not professionally written, people will accept the format of your message and not make much of it.

What To Takeaway

Email is a tool to communicate and get bits of information across from one person to another. If something is exceptionally urgent people will call you (but I even have tips for phone calls in the next chapter).

Treat checking email like a task in itself where you check, respond, and finish so you can move on to other things that are more important like activities that can move the needle and grow your business. Or even if you don't have your own business, time is better spent with your friends or family.

TIME THIEF 3: UNPLANNED AND UNSOLICITED PHONE CALLS

My favourite is when telemarketers call up and ask if you have 30 minutes to take a survey. No. You. Don't!

Phone calls, especially random unsolicited calls and wrong numbers are one of the most significant time wasters, and in this chapter, I will show you exactly how to take back control of your phone.

Why This Is A Big Problem

One thing that you will learn as the theme of this book and how you should run your life is that you need to protect your time like the oxygen you breathe. The other important thing to note is that others don't care about your time whatsoever, and will suck it up any which way they can to their advantage.

How You Should Be Taking Phone Calls

For you to get your time back, you need to operate in a whole different way; otherwise, nothing will change, and you will continue to feel that time is flying by and you are not in control. The following are methods you must incorporate so you can protect your most precious asset.

Keep Your Phone On Do Not Disturb

Most of the time anyway, you are getting marketing calls from 1800 numbers, wanting you to take surveys or sell you something you don't need, so why would you give them your time to take a survey when you get nothing out of it? There are hundreds of other people that are willing to sell time to answer their surveys, so you don't need to.

Also, why do you need to have your phone available all the time anyway, if someone needs to get a hold of you they will either leave you a voicemail or send a text message. And if it's family, then have them on emergency bypass on your iPhone, for example, that way their calls and messages will continue to come through.

You will begin to notice a sense of peace in your life when you have a phone that does not ding and ring at you at all hours of the day.

Return Calls At Specified Times

Go through your voicemail and call people back on your time, not theirs. Trust me, you will hear me say this over and over again in this book, people do not care about your time, and are more than happy to take any of it away from you.

When you do this, you are taking back control, and speaking to them when it's the right time for you.

Only Accept Incoming Calls That Are Scheduled

When you are planning a meeting with someone, ensure that they book a time with you in your calendar. This does a couple things, when you get the call, you are expecting it, you can be ready, and you can be focused on that person entirely. Otherwise, someone calls you out of the blue with a work issue, and you are not prepared.

Again, because this is already planned, you are not interrupted with a call you do not want to take.

Don't Ever Do Phone Surveys Or Questionnaires

Like I mentioned above, don't ever waste your time by giving it away to benefit someone else's needs such as telemarketers, or to answer surveys or questionnaires.

There are plenty of other people out in this world that do not value their time as you do, so they are more than willing to throw away their time doing tasks like these.

Utilize An Online Booking Software

Integrate an online booking calendar so you can send people a link to a system where they can then book online, and it is automatically added to your calendar, and this saves hours of time. It is linked to your Google Calendar for example, and will only show people available times, that way you can just give them a link and automate the entire process. You could save hours going back and forth, playing phone tag trying to book an appointment.

TIME THIEF 4: NOT SAYING NO

I took on too many projects I shouldn't have, worked with bad clients, and got nothing at the end of it. Now I look back and wish I had just said no on those occasions so I could have done something better instead, and I could have been more productive doing something else that would have gotten me further ahead.

Saying no to people has been the most liberating thing I have ever done and something you have to be able to do if you want to keep sane in your life and in business.

The Problem With Saying Yes

As I have said, people have their own agendas. And it's your job to always be mindful of what your goals in life are and stick to them.

When you feel bad when someone asks you to do something, that causes several issues, namely that you have now committed your time to something else. And that something is taking you and your time away from your main direction.

You Can Only Be And Do One Thing At A Time

When you agree to something and say yes, you are now bound to be at a particular place or do a certain thing. This prevents you from doing what you want to do, and be where you want to be.

You can't be everywhere at once, and you can't do everything at once, so if you keep saying yes to everything then you will continuously be drawn away from your objectives, and it will get harder and harder to say no next time.

Why You Need To Start Saying No

I noticed a considerable change in my life when I started saying no to people when they asked me for favours or to do something. I started being able to pick and choose what was right for me, not what was right for others. This allowed me to stay on my trajectory, and focus on my work and get things done a lot better - because now I had more time to focus on what I needed to get done, instead of being pushed and pulled in many different directions.

You Cannot Feel Bad

You are reading this book because you want to secure and protect your time, but if you say yes to everything people ask you to do, where does that leave anytime for you to work on you?

You have to learn to say no and not feel bad about it.

Saying no is not being rude, it's being strong, and confident that you have the right to do what you want to do with your time. And if it's not something you want to do, or it's going to cost you happiness or time or money in other areas of your life or work, you have to be firm and put your foot down.

Trust me, people will get upset - there is no avoiding this. People get angry because you are not fulfilling their plans. They absolutely don't care about your plans, so expect most everyone to get mad or upset when you tell them no. Once you understand this, you will find saying no a lot easier and not feel like you did something wrong.

You Get To Choose What You Want To Work On

When you say no, you are allowing yourself the opportunity to pick and choose. Not everything that comes your way in life is beneficial to you, and making a simple bad choice can be detrimental going forward. This is why it's so vital to be focused on your more valuable and longer-term goals continually, that way you can always assess a situation to see if it fits your direction or not and thus decide to accept or reject it.

It Gives You Time To Make A Better Decision

If you start off by saying yes to something, then you are committed, and most often it becomes too late to back out. But if you say no first, then if you later find that you do want to do something, you can most of the time go back and do it.

Saying no buys you time to make a better decision, often times we are asked to do something and simply put on the spot right then and there, with little time to think about the consequences, rewards, or repercussions.

TIME THIEF 5: MULTITASKING

Most people call it multitasking, I call it switch tasking, whatever you want to call it, multitasking is not real, and if you are doing it, you are doing yourself a great disservice.

So pretty much all you are doing when you think you are multitasking is just switch tasking, or jumping from one thing to another, and back again. This really does not work in life nor in business.

So why is that? Well, it boils down to the two concepts I speak of a lot: first - the brain can only focus on one thing at a time, second - it takes time for the brain to give you its full concentration when going from an existing task to a new task.

Still not convinced? Go for a walk down the street and then look down at your phone while trying to read an article on your cell phone genuinely. I would say in around 30 seconds your brain will be solely focused on the article you are reading and will then zone you out of what is happening around you, and therefore you will most likely be walking into someone very soon after that.

This is why a lot of cities now do not allow for talking on the phone while driving. Its because when you are talking on the phone, your brain focus and concentration is mostly on the call, and your attention to what is happening around you diminishes. This gets really dangerous when you look down at your phone or radio while driving, as I mentioned above within a very short time, your brain zones you out of the road, and your sole concentration goes towards you reading something on your phone, or trying to adjust the radio dial.

It Looks Great On A Resume

I have seen it on many people's resumes, including mine in the past. Yes, it looks good, something like, "Able to multitask and get many things done at once."

But seriously, do you? I think not, and let me explain below.

A Game To Prove My Theory

Grab a piece of paper, a pen, and a stopwatch. From here, get ready with your pen and paper to write down the 26 letters of the alphabet, along with the numbers 1 through 26.

You are going to do this test twice, and time yourself doing each of the following methods:

Method 1: Start the timer and start writing out the letters and numbers like this: A 1 B 2 C 3 D 4 E 5…etc until you get to Z 26, so you are "multitasking" between writing a letter than a number and then going back and forth.

Ok try that now and record your time.

Method 2: Ok so now instead of alternating letters and numbers you are going to write down all the letters in the alphabet first, then you are going to write the numbers 1 through 26 like this: A B C D E…etc to Z, then writing the numbers out like this: 1 2 3 4 5…etc to 26. Again time yourself doing this and record the time you did it in.

Ok, so how did you do? If you are like most, it took you longer to do method 1 than method 2, am I right?

How To Get Stuff Done The Right Way

Multitasking is terrible because the brain takes time to get "climatized" to what you are doing. And by you jumping back and forth, you are literally going to take longer to do something than if you solely focused on one thing at a time, completed it, and then moved on to the next thing.

Focus On One Task At A Time

Henry Ford literally invented the assembly line, some workers worked on numerous tasks on the car. He broke down the steps and realized there were 84 distinct steps to building the car. He then implemented that a worker did only one and only one of these steps, productivity went up, and he was producing vehicles at a record rate.

You see when you do one thing at a time and do it well, your brain can pour all its energy into that task. But when you start multitasking and try to do many different things at once, you are making it harder for the mind and body to adapt to the task at hand.

Chunk Your Work

As Henry Ford discovered, doing one task only allows your brain to get really good at doing one thing over and over again.

To add to this, one method that will also help you get more done in less time is chunking tasks.

You see, if you break up tasks throughout the day of similar nature, you again take longer to do them, but if you group related tasks together, then you can accomplish them much quicker because the tasks are similar in nature.

So for example, if you need to post something on Instagram, reply to a message on Facebook, and check your YouTube stats, group these tasks together and get them all done in succession in a time block called Social Media tasks.

This chunking of tasks keeps similar items together, so your brain doesn't have to take long to get refocused on those tasks as they are all similar in nature.

It Allows Yourself To Zone Into Deep Work

And this is why deep work is so powerful. When you focus on one thing, you can really get some good work done, but when you try to multitask, you going back and forth throws the brain off and it takes longer for it to reset back to the task at hand and reestablish the focus it needs to get that task done.

TIME THIEF 6: PERFECTION

Back when I ran my digital marketing agency, I wanted everything to be perfect, that's who I used to be - a perfectionist at heart.

Whether it was a beautiful website I was creating, or a blog post I was writing, or a marketing video I was editing, looking back now, I wasted so much time trying to perfect things that were already good enough.

It Sucks Up Your Time And Energy

Listen, perfection does a lot more than suck up the time out of your life, it also takes a lot of mental energy too.

You spend so much extra time trying to make something perfect, but then you really should ask yourself, is spending all that extra time trying to make something perfect going to make such a dramatic improvement? Most likely not.

I have something called the 80% rule. Get whatever I am doing to 80% quality, and then let it go, get it out to the world, just release it. That extra work, energy, and time I would have to spend to get it 100% "perfect" is not worth it, because almost no one would notice the extra work I did, and the return on my time would be negligible anyway.

The other thing to consider is that what is perfect to you is not perfect to someone else, as we have all heard the saying, "One mans garbage is another man's treasure."

There Is No Such Thing As Perfection

Why is it that we have this mentality that things, our work, and our lives have to be perfect before we can take the next step forward. Because it's all in your head, that's why. It's something we all individually have invented to justify why we can't be happy, why we can't move forward in our lives, why we can't achieve the next level of satisfaction. It's all man-made thoughts at the end of the day, so in essence, we are only trying to get things perfect for our own well being, but that type of thinking just holds us back.

Just Go For It

Wasting time on getting things to be perfect has no real benefits at all, and only prolongs your success.

Flush Perfection Out Of Your System

If you want to really make forward strides in life, get your time and life back, then flush perfection and the thought of it out of your mind.

You have to say to yourself that it's not going to hold you back anymore from doing anything, saying anything, or going somewhere.

It's the number one killer of peoples momentum, motivation, progression in life and in business.

It's like a bad habit, and it's now time to stop doing this habit for good.

Now Is The Perfect Time

The old Chinese proverb says, "The best time to plant a tree was 20 years ago. The second best time is now."

Stop wasting time contemplating when to do something, just do it now, see how the world reacts and then pivot from there. Otherwise, you are going to continue to be stuck in your head and not know what is on the other side.

The "perfect time" is the worst enemy to any human being and is no excuse to let life pass you by.

If you are not happy with something and want to break free from it - do it now.

If you want to achieve something, go on a trip, or do good for someone else - do it now.

We have no idea what tomorrow brings, so if you have the opportunity and the means to do something, then do it today. The last thing you want to do in life is to look back when you are older and have any regrets.

Get It Out To The World As Quickly As Possible

If you run a business, and you offer your customers products and services, the key is not to wait for those offerings to be perfect before you release them. The key is to get them out as quickly as possible so that way your market can tell you what they like, what they don't like, that way you can make improvements based on the market's feedback and not your assumptions.

Get your product and service offerings to that 80% good enough stage that I spoke about above, and then get it out to the world so you not only find out what works and what doesn't but you can also start to generate revenue for your hard work by allowing people to pay you back for what you have created.

TIME THIEF 7: BUSY WORK

I think back in the day I used to be the king of busy work for the longest time. Over my working career, though, I have come to realize the difference between productive work and busy work.

Busy work or what I would call "feel good" work, is work that you do to make yourself feel good that you are actually doing something at the moment, but it's not work that actually moves the needle in your business and life that gets you moving forward and ahead.

Why You Engage In It

In simple terms, busy work makes you feel good, they may be fun tasks that you don't mind doing. The problem with this is that when you do something that makes no difference to your life, you not only waste time, you prevent yourself from genuinely accomplishing great things.

It Doesn't Have A Place

When your planning is disorganized or not even organized at all, you are going to be very susceptible to wasteful busy work that makes no difference to your life or business in the long term.

The problem with busy work is that it doesn't have a place in your daily routine because it doesn't matter to your longer-term goals, so it is very easy for you to be working on something and then quickly get distracted with something else because you have no accountability to get that task done. If you focus on actual work though that does move the needle, you are more likely to put more effort and focus into it as you can now see how it relates to the bigger picture.

How To Eliminate Busy Work

Don't Dance Around Important Tasks

Only focus on tasks that move the needle in life and business. Stop doing stuff just because they are easy or make you feel good. A good indication of things you should be doing are the things you dance around doing. So many times, I found myself needing to do some essential tasks because I knew they were important, but I made some excuse in my head on why I should do this other random task instead. It didn't make any sense. I caught myself many times and have changed the way I do things now.

Ask Yourself Why

Why are you doing what you are doing? How does it relate to the bigger picture? Whenever you start a task, ask yourself this question, which will really make you think twice about whether this task is a waste of time or actually crucial to the longer term.

Always Plan Out Your Day In Advance

Plan out your daily tasks in advance. I do this the night before by planning out exactly what I am going to be working on the next day. This allows me to be clear on what needs to be done, so I don't wake up in the morning randomly doing things like busy work. This also allows me to ensure during my planning that what I have to do tomorrow is actually essential and related to the bigger picture and longer terms goals down the road.

Use A Project Management Software

Don't just start working on things during the day. Use a project management software to keep track of all your tasks. This does a couple of things, it shows you what you have coming down the pipe of things to do, plus it also gives you satisfaction to be able to check off completed tasks as you accomplish them.

Write down everything you are going to work on then you can clearly see what needs to be done, from there you won't be able to fit in useless busy work.

The formula is simple: plan what you need to do, then execute on your plan.

Most people start working and doing things with no bigger plan, which wastes a lot of your time on useless things. This slows down your momentum and productivity in life and in business.

TIME THIEF 8: NOT DELEGATING

Running my digital marketing agency taught me so many valuable lessons about life, and business, and especially time.

When I first started out, I did what most every other entrepreneur did, and that was wearing multiple hats, trying to juggle many balls up in the air at the same time without dropping anything.

Get More Time Through Other People

Then I started to drop the ball on things. And that's when I realized that I needed to bring on help. The first thing I did was to bring on someone who could act as an admin assistant, where they would be able to help with multiple general tasks. Right away, I felt a load off my back, as so many simple little tasks were now off my plate.

The light bulb went off, and I finally realized through this simple action what being an entrepreneur was all about. It's not about struggling to do everything yourself, not having any time left over to enjoy life. It's about stepping back and being able to be what I like to call myself as the captain of the ship, where I can see and have the vision on where I want to go and my team, or the crew, are the important ones that will help guide the entire ship there.

Delegating and having a great team of people around you gives you more time and much more freedom to do things you want to do and not things you have to do.

Even if you don't have your own business, having a private chef at home to make you your food can save you hours of time cooking, cleaning, and running around a grocery store shopping. What about a maid and cleaner that cleans up your place 3 to 4 times a week, just imagine being able to sit back and know that your home will be clean because you have a great system in place now to do that. Or what about your own driver, being able to offload the chore of dealing with traffic when you can sit back and learn something new or relax while someone else does the hard work makes you feel so much more relaxed and less stressful. And this is not about having boatloads of money to be able to afford a team like this. It is about planting the seeds in your mind so you can start looking at all that you do at home and at work and asking yourself, what can I delegate to someone else. Once you sit down and start seeing what you do daily, you can begin to see where exactly you can delegate and get more time back.

You don't want to spend all your time just doing simple tasks that can easily be outsourced to someone else to do. Doing all these little tasks adds up, and your time is better spent elsewhere.

Why You Need To Start Letting Go

No One Can Do It Better Than Me

The most often reason people don't let go and are not able to delegate tasks to others is that they feel that other people cannot do it as good as they can. I was like this as well, I was a perfectionist at heart and thought that no one would be able to do things to the level I needed them to be.

But then as I started slowly delegating, I saw that it was possible for others also to create great things and do them as I wanted. This was possible because I created systems of how I wanted things done, and by showing someone examples, then I would let them be and insert some of their creativity into the mix.

For you to get time back in life, you have to put this thinking aside for good; otherwise, you will lose precious time and a lot of wasted mental energy too.

You Cannot Scale Without Others

To be successful, you have to be able to delegate. I hit a point in my work and life where I felt like I wasn't able to grow. The reason for this was I maxed out on the amount of time I had in the day. The only way to scale up and to continue my personal growth and entrepreneurial journey was to bring on other team members and outside contractors to buy me time back, and by using their time and not mine, my abilities to scale were now limitless.

It's Not Your Job To Do Everything

Your job as an entrepreneur, for example, is not to do everything yourself, it's to have the vision of where you want to go. You create a talented team around you to fulfil that vision. Again, even if you don't have your own business, you need to see where it is you want to go in life and use the help of others to get you there. As I like to say, use your mind more and your hands less, which means use your imagination and vision to discover where it is you want to end up in life and in business and use the help of those around you to build you that vision with their hard work.

Find People That Are Better Than You

There are a lot of people that are better than you at specific tasks. I always looked for exceptional talent, because I knew there were so many people better than me at doing certain things. At the end of the day, I didn't really feel like doing accounting tasks, or web coding tasks, or video editing tasks. There are so many great people that have a passion for each one of these areas, and it was my job to surround myself with them and have them help me get to where I needed to go.

Always remember, it's not often good to be the smartest one in the room, the reason for this is that you cannot learn anything new. So always surround yourself with people that are better than you in specific areas and learn as much as you can from them along the way so you can improve yourself in life and in business.

Create A Training System Once

Create training documents, so you only need to teach someone once how to do something, because if they leave you don't have to reteach. I taught people, and then I would let them go, or our project would end, and they would move on, but then when a new project came back up, I found myself spending so much time retraining over and over again the same material.

This could be another area where you lose a lot of time is telling someone the same thing over and over again. Try to systemize your training material so that you could for example record yourself showing someone something on video and that way if you have a new person that comes on board they can just watch the video and learn everything they need. Do the work once and reap the benefits for it later as it does the work for you.

You Need To Separate Yourself From Your Business

For you to grow and scale your own business, you have to separate yourself from your work. The reason for this is simple, you only have 24 hours in a day, but you literally cannot work for that entire time, nor do you want to. For any business to grow it needs to be separate than the owner, so you have to get it to a point where you can step away for a months vacation for example, and your business is still making you money. You need to continually ask yourself if you can step away from your business, and will it continue to make you money if you do. If the answer is yes, you are in good shape, if they answer is no, then you need to look at why and how you can incorporate delegation or automation to be able to accomplish this to give you more time back.

TIME THIEF 9: PROCRASTINATION

As humans we love to procrastinate, we always tell ourselves that it's okay if we don't do something today, there is always tomorrow.

Unfortunately, procrastination is such a time thief because you simply waste so much time and effort trying to avoid doing things. The act of procrastination itself is an actual task that you perform, most often not even realizing it.

You have probably faced this yourself recently when needing to do something, simple things like throwing out the garbage or brushing your teeth, to more bigger things like sitting down to work on an important project or going to the gym.

You Don't Feel Like It

Putting stuff off usually means you don't want to do certain tasks, even though most often than not you should be doing them because they are good for you or add value to your life or business. Your brain and body are not in sync, and your body is telling your brain to take action, but your mind is saying that it doesn't "feel" like doing it.

This sucks up vast amounts of mental energy, which can take your focus away from other more important things.

How To Stop Procrastinating

Let's now take a look at a few ways I have successfully used to eliminate procrastination in my life once and for all.

Live Like There Is No Tomorrow

Live life like there is no tomorrow, seriously. If you allow yourself to make an excuse, you will naturally use it.

Work on creating this as a habit, the next time you need to do something but give yourself an excuse, say that there is no tomorrow and it must get done now.

An old proverb is that if you have a seed in your hand and you have the ability to plant it, do it now and don't wait because you don't know if tomorrow will ever come.

Tell Yourself There Is No Option

When I wanted to go to the gym, the voice inside my head would tell me that I am too tired, it would be more fun to watch YouTube videos and many other excuses.

When I started to then tell myself that I heard the excuses, but was not going to give them any power because it didn't matter what reason I came up with, there was no option to say no.

The voice in your head will keep trying to tell you to do other less important things always, but you cannot listen to that voice, you have to remind yourself that no matter what, you have to get this important task done without hesitation.

The 2 Minute Rule

If there is anything that is literally in front of you, like simple things as putting the dishes in the dishwasher, and it takes less than 2 minutes to do, do it right there and then. Because just imagine how many to do items you could add up to your task list that are super simple, super quick tasks. Just do them now and get them off your plate once and for all.

Treat it as automatic, if you see something that needs to be done, and it will take you less than a couple minutes to get it done, there is no point in keeping that task on a to-do list or in your mind, get it done and out of the way so you can focus on bigger more important things.

Break It Down

Sometimes you simply cannot get motivated to work on a project because things feel too big or too complicated.

You may have heard this one before, "How do you eat an elephant? One bite at a time."

Another big reason people procrastinate on projects is that they seem too big in your mind. The best way to deal with this is to break a bigger project into smaller and more manageable tasks.

Then just focus on getting the micro-tasks done one at a time, from there and after a short amount of time, you will start to see that these smaller tasks are bringing you closer to completing the bigger project and you will begin to get even more motivated to finish.

TIME THIEF 10: MEETINGS

Every day tens of millions of meetings go on around the world. The issue is that most of them end up not accomplishing anything and turn into a time waster for all parties involved.

A lot of people complain that meetings are not as productive as they should be so why is it that we are going into these important meetings yet coming out on the other side feeling like nothing got accomplished?

Why Some Meetings Are A Waste

The reason for this is two-fold. First, a lot of meetings try to cram too much into it and then end up not accomplishing anything. Along with this is that some regular meetings happen too often, and thus there is no real value being added as the last meeting was too close together.

The second reason, which is even more troublesome, is that there is a lack of focus, and therefore, no real actionable items come out from it.

Meetings interrupt into your deep work time, or what I like to call your Einstein time, that time where you are super focused, creative, and productive.

How To Have Better Meetings

Like anything else in life, you have to have a plan. Otherwise, you will end up going in different directions but eventually not getting anywhere. To have successful meetings that don't waste your time, you need to go in with clear objectives. But first, let's see if the next point may help quickly eliminate the meeting altogether.

Is The Meeting Even Necessary At All

Most meetings end up a waste of time for everyone involved as nothing actually gets accomplished. Is what you are meeting for able to be performed quickly over the phone or by email? This is why it is also useful to incorporate a project manager that everyone can be involved in. With this, all members are part of the project group and can see what tasks have been done and what tasks need to be done and can communicate through the project management system such as Teamwork or communication channels like Slack.

Look at your calendar now and start knocking off meetings that are not important to your ultimate goals.

Clear Purpose

This one is one of the most critical action items you can do right away to stop wasting time with your meetings. Have a clear purpose of what the outcome of the meeting is before the meeting with predefined written down goals and objectives. Otherwise, you can go end up in tangents. Send out your meeting material to everyone involved beforehand that way all parties understand the content of the meeting and have all the materials they need, that way no one comes to the meeting clueless about what it's going to entail or waste time looking for files or collateral required.

Set Time Limits

All your meetings should have a start and end time, simple as that. If you don't do this, you will be wasting a lot of time.

Furthermore, humans love to drag things out, if you don't set a limit to everything you will never get it done. If you give yourself 1 hour to do something, it often happens that you will take 1 hour to do that thing. So if you limit your meetings to a shorter time period, you will find yourself being able to finish a lot quicker and not waste so much filler time.

Not only should the meeting itself be limited, everyone should have an allotted time to speak around the table that way, no one drags on talking about useless information.

Limit Who Attends

If you don't need someone there, they should not be invited to the meeting. Meetings are about getting things figured out so that when you are done the meeting, there is better vision and a clear action plan.

A better way to communicate with them would be through the meeting notes or minutes. Have a notetaker take down the appropriate talking points of the meeting and then have this information shared with people that did not attend that way they can still get the information but didn't have to waste their own time just showing up to sit there.

Eliminate Socializing

Meetings are not supposed to be about who is doing what on the weekend or what they are eating for lunch. Eliminate useless socializing with your teammates and coworkers. Meetings are about getting things done, not socializing, if you want to socialize, then meet at a coffee shop after work hours.

TIME THIEF 11: ENDLESS TO-DO LISTS

This one had literally plagued me for such a big part of my life. I think I at one point used to have the record for the biggest task list on Earth. But why? The collection of things I needed to do became so large, I would obviously never be able to get to older items as the newer items would just stack on.

Task lists are like junk you throw into your garage. It's a recipe for disaster because if there is no clear plan on how to navigate the task list and get things off of it faster than things come onto it, you can clearly see that it becomes a losing battle, and the list will become bigger and bigger over time.

Why It's Come Down To This

Why as a society have we come to the point where we have so much to do that at the same time feel like we are not getting anything done?

The problem is we are not organized when you come up with an idea of needing to do something for a project or a task, you instinctively pop it into your to-do list, hoping to get to it later. What happens is it snowballs, and it gets buried down the list only to be another task that you will get to someday in your life with newer things continually piling on with no end in sight.

It Becomes Like Debt That Controls You

Endless task lists are like financial debt, after a while, you get used to a large number, and you then lose the ability to bring it down because the longer list becomes your normal. Along with this, it really does start to hold you down because you don't ever feel like you are making any forward progress.

It gets to a point where you check off one to do item and at the same time add 3 more so you get further and further behind to a list that becomes unmanageable and again, not only wastes a lot of your time trying to fight against it, but it consumes you mentally from the inside too.

Here Is How To Take Back Control

To get your time back, you need to initially focus on setting up the right system to manage your to-do list and the items on it. Below I will go through some of the best strategies I have developed to take back control of my to-do list along with my life.

Create Organizational Holding Buckets

Have a place set up to dump your thoughts and tasks. The biggest thing you can do right away to improve your productivity and get your time back is to get organized. Make that into a high priority task in itself. Because once you can sit down and create these organizational holding buckets, whether digitally or in real life, then you will be in such a better position to tackle little or big tasks.

One of my biggest wins was in setting up a project management system which helps me even for non-work related life items. What you want to do is within yours, create different projects based on how your business or life is split up.

So for work as an example, a project would be marketing, and within that project, you have task lists which are broken up into things like Email Marketing, Video Marketing, and Social Media Marketing. In each of these tasks lists, you can now add your tasks to, and each task has a home where you can place it for prioritizing it now or for getting to it later. So you are not just randomly dumping things all over the place like a napkin or in your head.

If you don't do it this way, you don't allow yourself to be able to segment items and give priority to them.

An example of what you can do at home is to break things up and group your buckets into compartments as well. For a simple example here such as Cleaning, Shopping, and Family. From there again go through and create task lists in the cleaning project such as Living Room, Washroom, and Bedroom, and you can list your individual to do items in each one of them there.

The whole point is to create a place where you can dump your thoughts so you can break things up for easy retrieval later as well as being able to prioritize them, so they don't just sit there forever but actually get completed as well.

Put Tasks Through Your North Star Filter

Your North Star is the place where you always focus on when you want to ensure you are going in the right direction in work and in life. It is your guiding light that tells you where you need to head towards.

By always asking yourself if something you need to do is of importance to your overall longer range objectives you may start to see that it is not, at which point you can begin to eliminate it from even wasting your time doing it in the first place and thus not taking up valuable time, mental energy, and task list space.

Understand That You Cannot Do Everything

Unfortunately, this life is very finite, and we don't have all the time in the world to do everything. You have to pick and choose your battles, and thus you have to narrow down your focus on the most important things by saying that if today was my last day on earth, what is the most important thing that I should be working on. That way you really narrow in on what's important related to the limited amount of time we have to do things not only during a day but from a grand scale of in life as well.

Start Chopping

Honestly speaking, a lot of the so-called tasks you put on your task list are not important enough to stay on there. Delete what is not urgent - because believe me if it's essential you will have to do it regardless even if it's not on your task list because life itself will remind you that it needs to be done.

Do Things Only Once

There are some things in life that you need to do over and over again that you can't get away from like taking a shower daily. But the problem with a lot of tasks is that we usually do things the first time, and then have to do them, again and again, a particular time later.

For you to be more productive, try only to do things once. So for example, if you have to train someone how to do something, why not create a video training program you can produce once that way you don't have to keep training new people all the time. As they join your company, for example, they would just watch your videos, and you won't have to keep spending your individual time with them as you have now separated yourself from time.

TIME THIEF 12: YOUR 9 TO 5 JOB

I was debating whether or not I should be putting this chapter in the book. The reason for this is that we all, including myself, need money to survive in this life. From home rent to groceries, to gas for your car, it's obvious that it costs money to live and thus we all need to work to earn income.

But I felt it was still vital to at least get you thinking about alternatives to what you are doing. At the end of the day, we are all stuck in daily ritual patterns, and until you stop doing what you are doing, take a step back and really analyze everything, things will continue to feel normal. But what I want you to ask yourself would be is that normal way of earning an income the best option for you and your family, and especially your time?

So What's So Bad About A Job Anyway

Trading time for money is one of the hardest ways to earn an income, and of the biggest lessons I took away from doing things in my agency where I was providing a service, and I myself was the business, so if I didn't work, then I made no money.

In this chapter, I want you to have an open mind about how you make money and how that relates to your time specifically because that way you can step back and really analyze if there are better ways to make an income. This book is not about quitting your job today and just starting a business - its about giving you the tools and the mindset to be able to protect your valuable time that is so limited as it is in your life, and constantly look for better ways to spend your time on things that truly mean something to you. This is about you having the time to do what you want and need to do in life, by you choosing where and what to spend your efforts on, and not by your circumstances having to dictate how and where you spend your time.

Your Job May Overlap Your Einstein Time

What I learned later in my life was that we all have what I call is your Einstein time. This is where you are most focused, productive, and energized. For me, this is from around 8am to 12 noon. The problem for me was that this time usually fell into with me having to be at a job. Those jobs took over my Einstein time and prevented me from working on my own entrepreneurial ventures when I was most productive and focused.

Commuting In Traffic Without Being Paid

You have to travel to get somewhere whether that be in your own car, the bus, subway, or train, you need to spend time just getting to this workplace location in which you are not getting paid at all, and you are travelling for free and not being compensated for this time.

Lack Of Vacation Time

The problem here is that if you don't have enough vacation days or have run out, you can only go away when most everyone else goes away, and prices are going to be higher such as the weekends or stat holidays. This also means places are going to be a lot busier and probably a lot more stressful with so many more people there.

Lack Of Free Time To Run Errands

You cannot just pick up and go to a doctors appointment or take your child to where they need to go, you need to ask for permission first as the job is blocking your time from being able to do regular errands.

When most things like doctors offices and the post office are closed outside of this time of the regular 9 to 5, so doing basic tasks needs you to take time off from work. Which may even mean you now instead of being close to where you need to go from home, you may be out of your way to get to where you need to go, and with a confined lunch break of 30 minutes, you cannot travel too far, unless you take a vacation or sick day.

Location Dependant

You physically have to be somewhere to earn income. You are locked away at a specific location for the majority of the day of mostly 8 to 9 hours, and for weeks and months to come.

How You Can Get Your Time Back From Your Job

Again, this is all about thinking about how you are spending your time currently, and looking at ways that may be able to help you get more of your precious time back.

One of the first ways to do this is that you need to start increasing your income streams. What this will do is allow you not to have to rely on your job alone for income solely, and eventually will allow you to buy your time back to do the things you really want to in life.

The only reason you go to a job in the first place is for the pay cheque every two weeks. If you can, however, replace that pay cheque with something else then there is no need to go to that job anymore.

Create Things That Separate You From Time

The whole point is to get your mind at least thinking of what more you can do to gain your time back so you can spend it doing important things like being with your family and friends.

Create A Book To Sell

One way to start generating income is to share information with others by means of an ebook or physical book. Look at things that you are passionate about in life and that you are good at. Other people would love to know what you know and also possess that knowledge to improve their lives. So why not bundle your expertise and write a book to sell to others. You can then post your book on websites like Amazon to get others to buy it, and you can make a royalty from the book on each sale.

Develop A Video Training Course

Again, selling information is one of the best ways to earn income, because you can bundle your knowledge and sell it to others who are craving to know what you know. Video is now one of the most types of consumed mediums, and video training courses allow you to not only talk about what you know but visually show people too. Things like healthy eating, how to stay fit, how to make a website and almost everything else under the sun. You are an expert at something, so why not sell that information and help others along the way. This saves you time because you no longer have to work to create a training program continually, you see, you work to create the content once, and then people can buy it over and over again without you having to keep investing time into it.

Sell Physical Products Online

The growth of e-commerce over the last few years has been unprecedented and with websites like Amazon being the giants of the commerce industry jumping in and being part of the action can allow you to get more time to focus on other things.

Getting into e-commerce, like selling on Amazon physical products with their program called Amazon FBA or Fulfilment by Amazon, allows you to sell things while you sleep. You simply ship your products to the Amazon warehouses directly, and then when an order comes in, Amazon picks and packs the item, as well as handles the entire shipping process out to the customer. So again, you can sell and earn profits at all hours of the day and night, and you don't even have to be there.

Focus On Selling Products Instead Of Selling Your Time

These are just a tiny handful of ways to earn an income without having to trade time for dollars continually. At the end of the day, it's about working once, and then creating something separate from your time that you can sell, whether physically or digitally. Products are so much better than services and jobs because with products you can earn income while you sleep, with services and employment, you physically have to commit time to earn income continually.

As the famous billionaire investor Warren Buffett said, "If you don't find a way to make money while you sleep, you will work until you die."

TIME THIEF 13: WAITING IN TRAFFIC AND LINEUPS

I can't imagine anything more frustrating than this one. Can you add up the time you actually had to wait in some form of line up or vehicle traffic this past week? I am sure if you start adding up the time, even if it is a few minutes here and there, it starts to really add up. And the problem is that it has become so normal just to be waiting around, that most people accept it and just let it be, not taking into consideration how much of their precious time is being lost.

In this time thief, I am not so much going to tell you how to eliminate waiting in line ups whether that be in your car or standing in line, but more so showing you what you can do not to let this time be so much of a waste.

Why This Is Going To Become A Bigger Problem Over Time

The world's population is increasing, and the traffic issues we have, especially on the road of a lot of cities globally is very apparent. Most often, you are stuck in rush hour traffic for 30 to 60 minutes just to go short distances.

This means a lot of added time that you are either sitting waiting in your car to get somewhere, or sitting at a doctors office waiting for your appointment.

Over time, however, line ups are just going to get busier and longer, and you need to be taking the right actions now to be able to ensure you are not just sitting and waiting around and letting your precious time pass by.

Things You Can Do While You Wait

Yes, I understand that sometimes waiting in line is unavoidable. This should never be an excuse to let this time be a waste. I want to show you how you can use this time to better yourself.

Self-education has been my greatest gift throughout my entire life. I have self-taught myself almost everything from web design and running a business to wellness and self-improvement.

I want you to continue to educate yourself each and every day, just like you are doing now by reading this book because the more information you can learn on different topics, the more it will benefit yourself and help your family live a better life.

Listen To An Audio Book On Audible

One of the best things you can do while you wait is to listen to audiobooks, especially while you are driving for more extended periods. Using this time to learn something new on health, wellness, self-improvement, business, finances, or whatever topics interest you would benefit you so much more than just listening to the radio commercials which gives you no benefit at all.

Audible is one of the best platforms for audiobooks, and no matter what topics you are interested in, you will most likely find an audiobook to help you learn something new.

Learn Another Language On Duolingo

Thanks to the internet, the world has become abundantly more connected, and no more are you dealing with people right next door.

The entire world is now at your reach, and learning a new language will give you the ability to connect with so many more people.

You are also able to gain a lot more confidence while travelling to new places while on vacation or for work. The key to learning a new language is repetition and consistency so you will want to keep practicing daily and immerse yourself within the language to be able to help your mind absorb the new language better.

Listen To An Informative Podcast

With the explosion of podcasts over the last number of years, there is nowhere you can turn without being able to gain self-education or online training.

Podcasts are also an excellent way to learn new things, often from a more conversational tone compared to audio books.

And with so many different channels to listen on, such as Apple Podcasts, Stitcher, and SoundCloud, there are plenty of podcasts to subscribe too.

One thing to note here is that there is also a lot of entertainment based podcasts, but what I am talking about is you subscribing to informative podcasts that provide you new knowledge and insight to better yourself in either life or in business.

Watch A YouTube Training Video

If you are going to sit on the train or the bus, use this time to learn how to be a better writer, how to get in better shape, how to make passive income, how to better your life in some way or form.

But whatever you do - do not use this time to watch useless videos on YouTube of people doing crazy things. Trust me that is not going to get you anywhere in life and will waste so much of your time as I mentioned in a previous chapter.

YouTube has been my go-to self-education tool for so many years, and I recommend to find what your passions are, areas in your life you want to improve, parts of your business you want to get better at, and then find a few channels that can get you to this higher level.

Like anything, things can be used for good or for bad. When I talk about YouTube, sure you will see that new music video pop up in the feed, but don't waste your time watching stuff like that. Develop a habit of just spending 20 to 30 minutes a day learning new things that can help you in the long term.

Always Ask Yourself What I Could Be Doing While I Wait

Don't let line ups be an excuse for allowing your time to pass you by. Instead, turn it around and use it as an opportunity to better yourself by learning something new, that is, in my honest opinion, the best investment that you can make for yourself.

TIME THIEF 14: HAVING TO GO PLACES

I recently got to a point in my life where I wanted to really become a digital nomad. I wanted to live a life of freedom where I didn't have to be somewhere to be able to earn an income.

I have also always loved to travel to new cities, and that is something I wanted to do more with my family.

Because of this, I have had to structure my life and business to be location independent. And because of this, it has forced me to live in different ways, to create systems that allow me to work from a laptop and with a wifi connection from anywhere in the world.

How This Got Me Thinking

As is the theme of this entire book, protecting your time should always be your top priority. I started to keep track of all the amounts of travelling I had to do to get to places around town, such as going out to get a carton of milk, or meet up with one of my business partners, and realized travel time takes a lot longer than we think.

Now, as I have mentioned in the previous chapter 13 above, I gave you the tools and mindset to be able not to waste this time. Yet in this chapter, I am going to take it another step further and show you how you can save time ultimately by limiting your travelling around town.

Save Time By Staying In

The less you have to do spending time on things you don't want to do or don't enjoy doing, and the more time you can spend on more enjoyable things will start to bring you a lot more happiness and less stress, along with more time on your hands.

TIME THIEVES

Order Groceries Online

I am not one who likes going grocery shopping in the first place. Most of the time, I feel like trying to find something is a needle in a haystack in some grocery stores. Along with the fact the line ups just to pay at some stores are horrendous.

Going to the grocery store can take 30 minutes just to go get milk. One of the best inventions in this space was when they came out with home grocery delivery that so many grocery chains now offer.

Simply pull out your phone, open your grocery chain app, and start adding items to your cart. When you are done and have everything, simply pay, and select a day and time for delivery and just sit back and wait. A personal shopper then goes around the store and picks up everything you requested and bags them up for you. From there, a delivery driver brings everything right to your doorstep, and often times directly into your kitchen.

We all have to eat, and this type of shift in how we shop for groceries is a game changer in my opinion.

Schedule Courier Pickups

Instead of having to go out to drop off packages and parcels, several couriers such as UPS can pick up directly from your home or office, so you don't have to go out and waste time in traffic.

Simply go onto the courier's website, and enter your pick up details and a courier driver will then come and pick up the parcel, scan it, and send it on its way.

Deposit Cheques Through Your Phone

Gone are the days of having to receive a cheque and needing to go to the bank to deposit it, many North American banks also offer online cheque deposits so you can simply take a picture of the front and back of the cheque and deposit it right from your phone. So if your employer, for example, still uses cheques instead of direct deposit, this improvement in online banking saves you time in this area.

Hire An Assistant

This may not be as expensive as you may think. But hiring someone to run your errands is a lifesaver. Even if you don't have a business, several people are fully qualified to be hired for a certain number of hours per day to run basic errands for you. What could be better than you enjoying a drink by the pool with your feet up and fully relaxed knowing that you have someone else dealing with traffic, congestion, and finding a spot in parking lots doing the work for you.

Have Online Meetings With Zoom

This one alone has saved me hundreds of hours of travel time, and I am a huge proponent of online meetings. So many times, I have had online meetings through Zoom with my business partners or have interviewed job candidates for positions I was hiring for. Zoom is the best tool for online meetings, and it doesn't have to even be in a business setting, you can video chat with people all over the world, share your screen, send files and so much more all for free.

It All Starts With Looking At Your Routines

I am not saying just always stay at home and don't go anywhere, I am saying that you need always to be thinking of better options if you can of allowing you the ability to have to avoid travelling to do errands as that time can really add up.

As with anything and what I will keep preaching, look at what you are doing, those regular things that are normal to you, and ask yourself do I have to go out to do this, or can I have someone else do it for me? Your time can be better spent doing more enjoyable things like spending time with your family and friends.

TIME THIEF 15: THE NEWS

I wanted to close off this book in this last chapter telling you about a big time waster that most don't assume to be one. Every single day, we are constantly bombarded with information coming to us from all different angles, have it be through the television, the internet, in newspapers, and magazines.

This news information about what could be happening locally or halfway across the world, I believe to be one of the big time thieves. This is because it's completely surrounded us in our day to day lives, and it is challenging to escape from it. It's become normal always to want to know what is happening and to consume news stories from many different channels and mediums.

Why You Need To Take A Step Back

It's time you become aware of how information is presented to you, as well as why that information is presented to you, that way you can become a better filter of what information you should be concerned about versus what information that you can ignore.

It's A Non Stop Overload Of Information

There is always something happening, and your brain is constantly being bombarded with information all day, every day, and this is all on top of marketing content you are getting from advertisers who are trying to sell you things.

So much of the news that happens does not even affect you, nor has anything to do with you, nor can you even control if it did affect you like an announcement of your taxes or gas prices going up.

This goes beyond just the news you watch on your TV, it's any type of news that comes in through the paper, the internet, on your phone, through an app, etc.

The information that is presented is not meaningful or relevant to you and your life, and you are not going to be doing anything with the information you watch anyway. News is only important if it directly has an effect on your own life, and most of the time, it doesn't.

New News Becomes Old News Very Quickly

The news changes daily. Just like social media posts, the news itself changes very rapidly and throughout the day.

What are headlines today, are totally forgotten tomorrow. The reason for this is that there is just too much information going around, if you are given a news story for too long, you get bored of it quickly, so news outlets have to keep it fresh by giving you new news daily to keep you hooked and coming back for more.

It is like a constant conveyor belt of information that never ends pouring into your brain, once the new news comes in, the old news is quickly forgotten as the news outlets don't bring it up anymore or focus on something more enticing as I will explain here next.

It's All Negative Because That's What Sells

Have you ever watched a reality show and it's filled with nothing but wall to wall drama? That's because negativity attracts humans more than positivity. It's human nature, and the same reason you slow down as you drive by an accident on the street.

It's the job of news outlets to give you disturbing or troubling information first, that's why most of the news channels you watch don't have any feel-good content until right near the very end of their programming.

News is a business at the end of the day, for TV they need viewers, for print they need readers because advertisers pay the bills, so there is always going to be news stories making the front page. Otherwise, outlets cannot make money.

It's also newspapers too, without you picking up the paper, they cannot sell ads space. Their job is to sell ad space priority first.

Paying attention to the news makes you negative, which lowers your willpower and makes you more depressed and stressed as you then feel you are not in control, and the world is going south.

This affects you emotionally too, as your aspect instead of seeing the world in a positive light where you can go out and achieve anything, now you feel like what is the point of doing anything if there is so much negativity. It goes beyond wasting your time, it destroys your emotions.

Positivity is vital to your success because positivity pushes you further in the distance, and that allows you to reach higher and do more and better yourself greater.

With negativity, it hooks you in to want more and to know more, and you end up in an endless negative loop.

Deal With What You Can Control

At the end of the day, you have to remain focused on your life and your own actions. Those are the only things that will help you get ahead in life. If your focus is always on what is happening around you, then your core will not be strong, and you will also be reacting to situations instead of taking the initiative for your life and taking the right actions to better it.

Avoid The News In General

The best way to gain your time back is to avoid seeking out the news whether that be in the evening sitting on your couch changing the channels trying to find something to watch, or while you are surfing online and find yourself reading what happened in the world today on a website.

One thing to add to this though is that if you are working in a field where news impacts your work, such as a financial analyst, then yes, it obviously makes sense to focus on news specifically related to the financial industry. You need to know that to do your job properly. But you can clearly see a line here that can be drawn to news that has an impact on you and that doesn't.

Don't Waste Your Time With Gossip Channels

This also goes for the morning talk shows. On a lot of radio stations, there is more talk than music. You usually get to hear about the latest gossip or usual garbage. Turn the radio off! Listen to a podcast, listen and learn a new language training, do something other than listen to useless chatter about something that literally makes no improvements to your life nor benefits you in any which way shape or form.

Others Will Fill You In

People say well if I don't keep up with the news, how can I know what is happening in the world. Paying close attention to the news is a complete waste of time.

Trust me, if something significant happened, your entire friends and family would ask you, did you hear about so and so? Other people will be your filter for what is worth knowing about or not.

It's not your job to be the informed citizen that always knows what's going on in town and around the world, because you have your own things to focus on and your own growth in life and in business to deal with.

Focus on what really matters in your life and business, and you will reach the success that you deserve.

ABOUT THE AUTHOR

 My name is Maher Abiad, and I am a master trainer and success coach who helps those who are motivated to achieve their absolute fullest in life and in business. My mindset training has helped hundreds achieve success in their lives and businesses through the confidence I have instilled in my students and clients through the knowledge of how to be the most productive they can be at all times. I have a passion for educating and inspiring people through the knowledge that I have gained over my career, and I love to share this information with everyone. Learn more about me, contact me, and hire me for consulting, and speaking engagements you have on my website at maherabiad.com

ONE LAST THING...

I would be very grateful if you would post an honest review of this book on Amazon. Your support really does make a difference to me, and I read all the reviews personally so I can get your feedback and make this book even better. This will also help other readers to know what type of information can be found in this book and what you got out of it.

Thanks again for all your support!

Maher Abiad

www.ingramcontent.com/pod-product-compliance
Lightning Source LLC
Chambersburg PA
CBHW072254170526
45158CB00003BA/1074